From SMOKE SIGNALS to EMAIL

MOMENTS IN HISTORY

by Shirley Jordan

Perfection Learning®

YA

Book Design: Amy Sharp
Cover Design and Production: Michelle Glass

Image Credits: Library of Congress pp. 23, 24, 26, 29;
All other images came from Art Today.

About the Author

Shirley Jordan is a retired elementary school teacher and principal. Currently a lecturer in the teacher-training program at California State University, Fullerton, California, she sees exciting things happening in the world of social studies. Shirley loves to travel—with a preference for sites important to U.S. history.

She has had more than 50 travel articles published in recent years. It was through her travels that she became interested in "moments in history," those ironic and little-known stories that make one exclaim, "I didn't know that!" Such stories are woven throughout her books.

Printed in the United States of America. For information, contact
Perfection Learning® Corporation, 1000 North Second Avenue,
P.O. Box 500, Logan, Iowa 51546-0500.
Tel: 1-800-831-4190 • Fax: 1-712-644-2392
Paperback ISBN 0-7891-5144-8
Cover Craft® ISBN 0-7807-9315-3

TABLE of CONTENTS

A TIMELINE of IMPORTANT EVENTS

Before 1639 and after — American Indians communicate using runners, sign language, torches, and smoke signals.

1639 — In Cambridge, Massachusetts, Stephen Daye establishes the first printing press in the American colonies.

1704 — The *Boston News-Letter* is published.

1741 — The first magazine in the colonies, the *American Magazine*, appears in Philadelphia.

1773 — In California, Father Serra obtains a **franking**, or free, system of mail delivery for the Spanish missions.

1783 — The first daily newspaper in America, the *Pennsylvania Evening Post and Daily Advertiser*, is founded in Philadelphia.

1828 — Noah Webster publishes the first American dictionary.

1844 — Samuel F. B. Morse sends the first telegraph message.

1847 — The United States issues postage stamps.

1858 — United States letter boxes begin to appear on street corners. Americans no longer have to mail their letters at the post office.

The Butterfield Overland Mail Stage delivers mail to the West.

1860   Pony Express service begins.

1862   Snowshoe Thompson begins his mail deliveries over the Sierras to link Sacramento, California, to the miners in Nevada.

1863   The United States establishes a uniform rate for postage, regardless of distance.

1864   The railroads begin to carry mail. The test run is between Chicago, Illinois, and Clinton, Iowa.

1867   Christopher Sholes, Carlos Glidden, and S. W. Soulé build the first working typewriter.

1873   The first United States postcards are issued.

1876   Alexander Graham Bell invents the telephone.

1878   Sir William Crookes invents the Crookes tube, which produces **cathode rays**. This is the first step in the development of television.

1894   In California, carrier pigeons deliver mail to and from Catalina Island.

1894   Guglielmo Marconi invents the wireless telegraph.

1915   The first **transcontinental** phone call is made.

1918   The world's first regular airmail service begins between New York City, Philadelphia, and Washington, D.C.

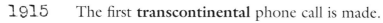

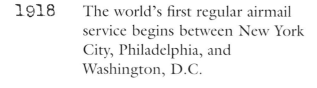

1920	KDKA broadcasts the first scheduled radio program.
1923	Pictures are televised between New York City and Philadelphia.
1928	WGY in Schenectady, New York, becomes the first station to offer regularly scheduled telecasts. It shows programs three afternoons per week.
1939	Millions see television for the first time at the New York World's Fair.
1941	Commercial television begins in the United States.
1947	The United States Postal Service uses helicopters to move mail from airports to post offices.
1951	The first coast-to-coast television broadcast shows President Truman opening the Japanese Peace Treaty Conference in San Francisco.
1953	The Postal Service begins moving some regular mail by airplane.
1962	A satellite transmits the first television images across the Atlantic.
1969	Scientists at UCLA meet to develop a system leading to the Internet.
1972	The first email message is sent.

chapter 1

SPREADING the WORD in EARLY AMERICA

The American Indians had many ways of announcing important events and telling ideas.

Sometimes they sent runners from village to village. Other times they signaled by waving animal skins. Some traded messages by catching the sun's rays on mirrors made of shiny **mica**.

Often hunters wanted to keep from making noise. So they talked to one another with hand signals.

Often they met others who were strangers. The strangers usually spoke different languages. So they used hand signals called *sign language* to tell who they were. Indians from every tribe understood hand signs for terms like *peace* or *help*.

Fire was often used for signals too. Sometimes men stood high on a hill holding up torches. One torch might carry a certain message such as "An enemy is coming." Two or more could mean something else.

But the American Indians had another favorite way of using fire to send messages. It was the smoke signal.

Let us join Little Deer, an Osage Indian boy. His father is about to teach him to communicate this way.

———————◆•◆•◆———————

Little Deer's father was Running Stag. He led his son to the hill high above their village. Under his arm he carried a bundle. It contained branches of oak, ash, elm, and long-burning hickory.

It was a clear, sunny day. Little Deer carried a bundle too. He climbed steadily. He was happy that his father was taking him to the signal hill.

Little Deer scrambled over the rough rock. It felt warm under his bare feet.

At the top, Running Stag put down his bundle of wood. He nodded to Little Deer.

"Open your bundle," he said. "We will soon need the milkweed and dandelion fuzz you gathered. Those will help us start the fire."

Little Deer unrolled the animal-skin blanket. Besides milkweed and dandelion, it was filled with other **tinder**. There were bits of bark, pussy willows, and dry needles.

The boy watched his father pile hickory sticks on the rock ledge. Then Running Stag added some of the other wood.

Running Stag pointed to small spaces between the branches. These were places where Little Deer would tuck bits of tinder. They would be needed as soon as his father had made a spark of fire.

"There are white men coming in a wagon," his father said. "They may be friends. Or they may not be. But we must let the other villages know. Then they can be ready."

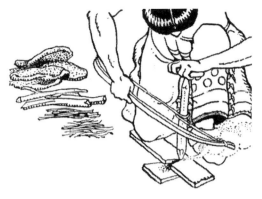

Running Stag unwrapped another bundle. He took out his hand drill. It was a pointed wooden stick.

"Now I will teach you to make the fire, my son," he said. He placed a piece of cloth on the ground. It was much smaller than his blanket.

On top of it went a flat block of wood. Small holes on top showed earlier burning.

Running Stag placed the point of his drill stick upright into one of the holes. Then he began to roll the drill stick back and forth.

Faster and faster he rolled the stick with the bow. Little Deer watched carefully.

In a few minutes, wisps of smoke rose from where the two pieces of wood met. Little Deer crept closer.

"Is it time?" he asked.

"Yes," said his father. "Just watch for a spiral of smoke. Under it will be the spark of a tiny hot coal. Hold a bit of dandelion fuzz near it. Then move the burning bit to the cloth."

In a few minutes, a tiny fire was burning brightly on the cloth. Running Stag lifted the cloth gently. He shook the sparks onto the branches and tinder he had prepared.

Little Deer watched as the fire grew larger and brighter.

"I hope some day I can do that as well as you do," he said softly. His father smiled.

They added more wood. The fire began to crackle, and flames stretched upward.

Running Stag unwrapped a deerskin. Inside were some grasses that grew near the village. The grasses were well-soaked in stream water.

Little Deer helped his father place the wet grass on top of the fire. At once, the bright fire was hidden in a huge plume of smoke.

Little Deer choked as the smoke reached his throat. He jumped back. His eyes burned, and he felt tears on his cheeks.

Finally, he could see again. His father was shaking out one of the animal skin blankets.

"Now you must help with the message," he said.

Little Deer held two corners of the blanket. His father stood on the other side of the fire. He held the other two corners.

Running Stag lowered the blanket over the smoking fire. His son lowered his end too.

Cover, raise, cover, raise. Running Stag made the smoke signals tell a story. Little Deer followed his father's lead. Sometimes they stopped for a while and let the flames burn brightly again.

Then it was time to add more wet grasses to the fire. For many minutes, they repeated the smoke signals. The puffs that rose into the sky told the message, "White men are coming your way."

Little Deer would remember this day forever. He was proud that his father had taught him to make smoke signals.

chapter 2

COMMUNICATION
in the COLONIES

Americans had an interest in communication even before 1776. A few newspapers and magazines served the colonies.

The colonists had left behind a simple mail-delivery system in England. But bad roads and slow horses delayed deliveries.

Service was no better in the New World.

Leaders of Our Nation's Early Postal Service

Andrew Hamilton became the first Postmaster General of the colonies in 1691. But the colonists were not happy with the service's rules. Postage cost a lot. And inspectors could open the mail. They searched for any words that were against the king.

The colonists organized against England's rule in 1775. The Second Continental Congress made *Benjamin Franklin* our nation's first Postmaster General. Franklin had earlier served as Co-Deputy Postmaster General of the colonies from 1753 to 1774.

President *George Washington* wanted an efficient mail service. He helped survey the newest post roads. In 1782, the Continental Congress guaranteed that no private letters could be opened or delayed by the post office. This new liberty was popular with the people.

Samuel Osgood became the first Postmaster General under the Constitution in 1789. There were 75 post offices. But fewer than 2,000 miles of roads connected the mail service. Much expansion of the mail service was needed.

A Postal System for the West

A system of mail delivery existed in the West before 1776. Military messengers in Spanish California carried packets of mail each month. They traveled between Monterey, California, and Loreto at the southern tip of the Baja peninsula. It was a 1,500-mile journey.

Much of this system had been developed by Father Junípero Serra. He was head of the Spanish missions in California.

In 1773, the Viceroy of New Spain gave Serra the right of franking. This right was given to all priests in the mission system.

Spanish messengers started from the San Francisco area, the first of each month. They traveled south. Mail was collected at each mission and small village.

The messengers emptied their bags of mail, called *mochilas,* when they reached Loreto. Then they turned and headed back north. This time they carried mail from Mexico and Europe.

Except for those coming from the priests, there were not many letters. Most of the people living in early California could not read or write. Los Angeles, for example, was then a town of 200 people. But only five or six of them knew how to write.

Time passed. The United States had defeated Mexico in 1848. And it claimed land that included California. Now the mail was a government responsibility.

A strange method of mail delivery developed in Los Angeles about this time. Wilson and Packard were merchants with a store on Main Street. They set a large tub at the end of one counter in their store.

All the mail addressed to Los Angeles went into the tub. People who expected a letter sorted through the tub to see if their message had come.

Colonel John Wheeler later owned the store. He continued the tub-mail system.

But in 1850, a stern postal official from San Francisco arrived. He discovered this casual method of mail delivery.

ROUTE BETWEEN MONTEREY AND LORETO TODAY

"This is no way to move the mail of the United States government!" he shouted at Wheeler.

Wheeler was insulted. He told the man to take the mail somewhere else. He could no longer be bothered with it.

Now an official post office was needed in Los Angeles.

The office opened on April 9, 1850. The building was an improvement. But mail service was no better.

Letters that *did* come were very precious. Patrons packed the post office after each delivery. The postmaster sorted the letters. Then he called out names and addresses. Those waiting answered with a shout and a wave of the hand. Then the letter would fly through the air into outstretched hands.

No one seemed to object to this "pitch and toss" method of delivering the mail. It lasted for many years.

chapter 3

The ARTIST Who TURNED INVENTOR

Samuel Finley Breese Morse was born in Massachusetts in 1791. He was the oldest son of a minister. Samuel's father had written the first American geography book.

Young Morse loved to draw and paint. He would often sketch pictures instead of doing his lessons. His parents found it hard to control him.

The boy was very bright. But he was always in trouble over his unfinished lessons. Reverend Morse didn't want his son to be an artist. He had other plans for him.

Young Morse began his studies at Yale. His father had attended this college. But Samuel was still not ready to settle down.

His only interest seemed to be in drawing. But he did pay attention in his science classes. His professors were working with electricity. Their lectures on that exciting new subject held his attention.

Will electricity someday be used in people's houses? he asked himself. The idea truly seemed impossible.

Morse went home after college. Days he worked in a bookstore. Nights he painted. Sometimes friends paid him to paint their portraits.

But Morse dreamed of crossing the sea to England. That was where the fine art teachers were.

His parents finally saw how much he wanted to paint. They gave Morse as much money as they could. He could follow his dream of studying art in England if he used the money wisely.

He set sail from New York to London on July 15, 1811. The crossing took 22 days.

Morse liked everything about London and his classes. His letters home did not reach his parents for four long weeks. But he wrote often. He told about all the things he wanted to paint.

His father wrote back. He reminded his son that he would soon have to earn money. Why not paint portraits in England? People liked pictures of themselves. And it was a way to make money.

Morse knew his father was right. But first he wanted to try other kinds of art.

He carved small ivory figures. And he modeled with clay.

Morse was good at these projects. But he could not earn much. It was not nearly enough for a house and food.

His funds grew more and more scarce. Morse came home after just two years of study. Now he was ready to paint portraits.

But no one rushed to his studio. So Morse went from door to door and from town to town. A few people became his customers. But he longed for more.

While waiting for more art business, Morse turned to his interest in science. He invented a water pump for fire departments. It was not a success. Neither was a machine that cut marble.

Morse married during these years. He and his wife, Lucretia, had three children.

Morse traveled about New England. He painted as many portraits as he could sell. Lucretia and the children stayed with his parents.

Lucretia died of heart trouble in 1825 after seven years of marriage. Morse was filled with grief. He left his children with their grandparents. He had heard of a new chance to paint.

Congress wanted four huge paintings for the **rotunda**. Morse longed to be one of the artists.

He had to wait to learn which artists would be chosen. So he traveled through Italy, Switzerland, France, and England.

In France, Morse became fascinated by the **semaphore**-telegraph system. Tall platforms were built several miles apart.

The rotunda is a large central room in the center of the United States Capitol building. It is directly under the the dome of the building.

One man stood on top of a platform and held up two flags. The man on the next tower studied the position of the flags. He then repeated it for the next platform. Of course, the system did not work when the weather was bad.

Morse wondered if electricity could be used for a semaphore system.

In October 1832, he sailed home. Morse met some men of science on the ship *Sully*. He talked with them for hours about electricity.

Morse had an exciting idea. He would wrap wire around a nail and attach it to a battery. This would send electricity through the wire.

Why couldn't someone tap out a message at one end of the wire? he thought. Then a pencil attached to the other end could print the code.

Morse began work on such a code.

He was sure his idea about sending messages through an electric wire would work. He would go home and try to make it better.

Morse spoke to the ship's captain as he left the ship. "Well, Captain," he said, "should you hear of the telegraph one of these days, as a wonder of the world, remember the discovery was made on board the good ship *Sully*."

When Morse reached home, he was disappointed. He was not to do a painting for the Capitol rotunda. John Quincy Adams was a member of the selection committee. He had convinced the other judges that no American painter was good enough for the assignment.

Morse had no money. So he moved into a small room in a building owned by his brothers. There he lived, cooking for himself and working on his telegraph.

Morse did not know that the year before, another man had invented an electric telegraph in Albany, New York. But Professor Joseph Henry wanted to study some more. So he had not applied for a patent.

Morse continued to work on his invention. And he did apply for a patent. He just wished he could become rich enough to spend all of his time painting!

Morse rigged up a picture frame, a table, and some lead pieces to build his first telegraph. But he did not keep working on it.

He went back to his painting. The telegraph **receiver** sat, gathering dust, in a corner of his brother's home.

He took a position with the University of the City of New York. Pupils came to him to learn painting and sculpture.

Morse also taught photography for a while. He could see this was another way of creating portraits. He taught it using an amazing new device called the ***daguerreotype***. It etched pictures on a silvered copper plate.

One of his students was a young man named Matthew Brady. He later became world famous for his photographs of the Civil War.

Finally, Professor Leonard Gail from the university took a look at the telegraph invention. He had many ideas for improvements. He became Morse's partner.

Then former university student Alfred Vail helped with more good ideas. He, too, became a partner.

The three men improved the invention.

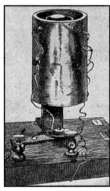

Now it had a notched metal rod to send messages. And it worked quite well.

The code Morse decided on was a series of dots and dashes. They stood for every letter of the alphabet and all the numbers from 0 to 9.

But still the telegraph had not been fully tested. Morse needed money for that. The government would not give him any. Neither would the English nor the French. No one was interested.

So Morse used his teaching salary and worked by hand. He and his two partners prepared a demonstration in 1842.

Morse waterproofed two miles of wire. He wrapped it with sticky tree pitch, tar, and rubber. Then he laid it under the water. It stretched from New York City's Battery Park to Governor's Island.

A ● ▬
B ▬ ● ● ●
C ● ● ●
D ▬ ● ●
E ●
F ● ▬ ●
G ▬ ▬ ●
H ● ● ● ●
I ● ●
J ▬ ● ▬ ●
K ▬ ● ▬
L ▬▬
M ▬ ▬
N ▬
O ● ●
P ● ● ● ● ●
Q ● ● ▬ ●
R ● ● ●
S ● ● ●
T ▬
U ● ● ▬
V ● ● ● ▬
W ● ▬ ▬
X ● ▬ ● ●
Y ● ● ● ●
Z ● ● ● ●
1 ● ▬ ▬ ●
2 ● ● ▬ ● ●
3 ● ● ● ▬ ●
4 ● ● ● ● ▬
5 ▬ ▬ ▬
6 ● ● ● ● ● ●
7 ▬ ● ● ●
8 ▬ ● ● ● ●
9 ▬ ● ● ▬
0 ▬▬

Unfortunately, not everyone on the waterfront knew about Morse's underwater cable. A ship's anchor caught the wire and tore it.

With the wire in two parts, no message could be sent.

Newspaper stories had brought crowds of people to see the experiment. They went home when there was no message. They wondered if the whole thing had been a hoax. They felt cheated. Had Morse played a mean trick on them?

Morse made one more try to interest Congress the next year. To his great surprise, he was awarded $30,000 to test his telegraph.

This time Morse strung his telegraph line from a Supreme Court room in Washington, D.C., to Baltimore, Maryland.

On May 24, 1844, Morse stood before a large group of spectators and tapped out a series of words. They had been suggested by the young daughter of a friend. Morse sent the message "What hath God wrought?" using his dots and dashes.

Now Morse was known and respected all over the world. He had wealth and fame. Rulers of other nations pinned medals on him. A statue of him went up in New York City's Central Park.

Samuel F. B. Morse had captured a dream while traveling on the ship *Sully*. And he had turned that dream into an invention that would transmit some of history's most important news.

chapter 4

MOVING the MAIL by SEA

The postal service in the eastern states was growing quickly by the middle of the 1800s. Mail was delivered more efficiently.

But not much had changed for those in the West. There was no good way to move the mail west, especially for great distances.

Coastal Packets

Ships called *coastal packets* began moving the mail between New York and New Orleans during the 1830s. People who lived near the Mississippi could send their letters down the river on small boats or barges. Then larger ships carried the mail around Florida and up the eastern coast. The trip took 14 days.

The Clipper Ships

But it took even longer for mail to reach the West Coast. Clipper ships began carrying mail and passengers from New York in 1845. They sailed around the tip of South America up to San Francisco.

These swift ships had trim lines and three high masts. They could be rigged with as many as 35 sails. But the trip took 89 days, 8 hours. Too long! Something had to be done to move the mail much faster.

Across the Isthmus of Panama

An answer was found on a narrow strip of land in Panama. It was an area called an *isthmus*.

Beginning in 1849, the Isthmus of Panama became an important route to California. The gold rush had begun. And people wanted to get there in a hurry.

Ships sailed from the Atlantic coast, carrying gold prospectors to Panama. They also carried mail.

Then both mail and prospectors crossed the isthmus to the Pacific coast on mules. They took another boat to California from there. It was faster than a clipper ship. But this mail moved slowly too.

chapter 5

The MAIL TRAVELS by LAND

Within a few years, letters were being carried over land as well. Three important services were the Butterfield Overland Mail Stage, the Pony Express, and the newly finished railroad lines.

The Butterfield Overland Mail Stage

Pioneers and miners who had gone west to search for gold were angry. They longed for news of home. Had they been forgotten? Something had to be done.

Businessman John Butterfield signed a contract with the government on September 16, 1857. He promised a twice-weekly mail service between St. Louis and San Francisco. The government agreed to pay him $600,000 a year. That was a huge sum in those days!

News of the contract was met with shouts of joy from the westerners. But it would be a full year before they saw any action.

On September 16, 1858, a Butterfield stagecoach pulled out of St. Louis, Missouri, and headed west. It had been one year to the day after the signing of the contract.

Another stage left San Francisco at the same time. It traveled east. The route stretched 2,800 miles. The trail was dotted with 180 stagecoach stops.

The coaches were pulled by teams of four or six horses. Six were needed when the going was steep and rough. Teams were changed often, usually every 12 to 30 miles. Sometimes mules were used instead of horses.

Mail was the main reason for the Butterfield Overland Mail Stage. But soon passengers were served too.

As many as nine people could buy tickets to ride inside the bumpy coach. Those who could hang on to the outside were charged ten cents a mile. The stages traveled about 12 miles an hour.

A one-way fare was $150. No food was served. Most passengers brought their own. They just hoped they had enough for the 24-day trip.

Sometimes meals could be bought at stage stops. But there were no guarantees.

Such a meal would likely have been dried beef and biscuits. A watery goat stew might be cooking on certain days. And a rabbit might be simmering with potatoes if hunting was good. Thick black coffee was sold at most stops.

The Butterfield Stage lasted three years. It used 100 coaches, 600 mules, and 1,200 horses.

Traveling by stagecoach was not for the weak or comfort-minded. Many of those making the trip in one direction decided to return another way. They usually sailed home on a clipper ship.

The Pony Express: Adventures in the Saddle

An ad appeared in the *Alta California* in March 1860. This was a leading newspaper for the growing population on the West Coast. The ad was about a new venture called "The Pony Express."

California had become a state ten years before. The population had grown from 20,000 to 500,000. And this had happened in a little more than five years.

The people on the West Coast were hungry for news. What was happening in Washington, D.C.? And what about the eastern states?

It took three months for mail and cargo to travel by boat around the tip of South America. A stage could deliver a letter in 24 days. But it still cost a lot. And it was only that fast if the letter was addressed to San Francisco. Something had to be done to speed communication.

A high-spirited, adventurous man named William H. Russell owned a shipping firm. Russell and his two partners, Alexander Majors and William B. Waddell, proposed a plan.

The men would use an overland system of riders and horses moving at full speed. Then their Pony Express would deliver mail in only ten days!

The idea was exciting. Soon the government gave the three men a contract. The Pony Express would deliver mail between St. Joseph, Missouri, and Sacramento, California. It would cover a distance of 1,966 miles.

Hundreds of young men answered the ad for riders. Eighty of those were chosen. These adventurers promised to go through burning desert heat. They would face fierce blizzards. And wild animal attacks. Even Indian raids.

Russell and the others built 165 stations along the route. These stops were not fancy or especially comfortable. They were just simple huts.

There a rider could change horses about every 15 miles. Most horses could no longer go at full speed after that distance.

The distance covered by the rider himself, however, differed. It depended on the kind of ground to be ridden. A route might be 120 miles across the flat plains. But a rider might go only 50 miles in the steep mountain passes. Then another young man took his place. The new rider would gallop off on a fresh horse with the mailbag swinging.

The job was exhausting. Sometimes young riders fell asleep in the saddle. But the ponies could be trusted to continue on their way.

One young rider was Thomas Owen King. He recalled a ride of 80 miles in which he reported to the station master that he had not passed Henry Worley. He was the horseman coming from the other direction.

King later said, "Worley had reported the same thing about me at the other station. We had both been sound asleep in our saddles. I guess we never knew when we passed each other."

The Express riders were a colorful cast of characters. They faced many dangers as they crossed the country. Their stories tell of the adventure and daring of the Wild West.

It was a rough life. But remarkably only one rider was ever killed on duty.

Several of the riders later became famous. The youngest rider ever chosen for the job was William F. Cody. He was later known as "Buffalo Bill." Cody was given a 116-mile assignment. He was only 14 years old.

Once his relief rider didn't show up. Cody took his place. This meant covering 76 extra miles.

When he had finished his round-trip ride, Cody had covered 384 nonstop miles. He left the saddle only long enough to change horses. Cody holds the record for the single longest ride in Pony Express history.

James Butler Hickok later became famous as "Wild Bill." He also worked for the Pony Express.

But he was not hired as a rider. His job was to tend the horses at one of the stations.

Hickok is not listed among the 120 riders. But he sometimes jumped into the saddle when he was needed. He took the place of an absent rider, thundering down the trail.

Work on a railroad that would run from coast to coast had begun in July 1861. Telegraph stations were added along the way. The space between telegraph stations grew shorter as construction crews finished the miles of track. Now there were more places where westerners could send or receive messages.

This meant less and less distance to be served by the Pony Express. Fewer and fewer customers used the service during the early months of 1861.

Longest Ride

Buffalo Bill Cody is credited with making the longest nonstop ride. When his relief rider didn't show, Buffalo Bill didn't stop for a break. He continued to the next home station.

Pony Bob Haslam is also credited with the longest ride in Pony Express history. But he stopped for a break. He slept for nine hours at Smith's Creek before continuing west.

The distance for both men's rides is not certain. Both have been listed as riding 384 miles. And both have been listed as riding fewer miles.

But one thing's for sure. Both men were dedicated to delivering the mail.

Finally on October 24, 1861, the first telegram was wired from San Francisco to Washington, D.C. The Pony Express riders were no longer needed.

The company came to an official end two days later. The Pony Express had lasted only 18 months.

A writer for the *California Pacific* newspaper wrote the following.

> *Summer and winter, storm and shine,*
> *day and night, he has traveled like a*
> *weaver's shuttle back and forth til*
> *now his work is done. Good-bye,*
> *Pony! You have served us well.*

The Railroads Move the Mail

The United States Post Office began operating its first railway mail cars in 1864. The test run was made between Chicago, Illinois, and Clinton, Iowa. Thousands of people watched.

Letters waited at the station in mail sacks in each city or town along the railroad line. These sacks were put on the railway mail car. Then while the train sped down the track, clerks in the mail cars sorted the mail for delivery to the next city.

Mail service had improved at last!

chapter 6

SNOWSHOE THOMPSON DELIVERS the MAIL

In 1862, a farmer near Sacramento heard news that made him angry. The government would no longer be delivering mail across the Sierra Nevada in winter.

The snow might be 60 feet deep in the mountains. But John Thompson didn't think that was any reason to stop service. He had lived his early years in Norway. No one there was ever stopped by snow.

Thompson put away the "bear paw" **snowshoes** used by his neighbors. He remembered how he had traveled as a boy. So he made himself a pair of "Norwegian snowshoes." These were much like ten-foot skis. And he held a long balance pole. It was like those used by tightrope walkers.

Thompson began delivering the mail while waiting for a government contract. Up the mountains he pushed. Sometimes for days. Then back down he soared with the ease of an eagle.

Thompson carried letters between Sacramento and the Nevada mines. Each trip was 90 miles. He also delivered clothing, food, and mining supplies for 50 cents a pound. Often his load weighed 100 pounds.

Snowshoe Thompson traveled without blankets. He used his Norwegian skills. At night, he made a lean-to or found a small cave or hollow log. Crouching close to his fire, he passed the nights without freezing.

Each night, he planned his route for the next day. He used the stars as his guide.

His eating habits were simple. Everything he needed was in his pack. There was usually some beef jerky and **hardtack**.

Thompson was the only link between California and the United States government during the Civil War.

Along his route, Thompson delivered medicines to the sick and injured. And he kept the miners in Nevada supplied with tools.

Snowshoe Thompson made two to four trips over the mountains each winter month for nearly 20 years. He plowed through blizzards and braved avalanches. Wild animals were always a threat.

Even though he had been promised a government contract, he never received one. He lived off the earnings from his small farm. He tried for years to collect back pay.

Thompson was still waiting for the government to pay him when he died at the age of 49.

chapter

The MARVELOUS MACHINE of CHRISTOPHER SHOLES

Christopher Latham Sholes was born in a log farmhouse in 1819. Our country was still very young.

Sholes began learning to become a printer when he was 14 years old. He worked hard. He had become editor of a newspaper by the time he was 19. It was called the *Wisconsin State Journal*. That same newspaper is still being published today.

Young Sholes liked to **tinker**. He loved to take things apart. But he loved to put them back together even more.

Sholes invented a machine with a good friend Samuel Soulé. It could print numbers on railway tickets. Soon he and his friend had improved it. Now their machine could number pages in a book.

They showed their numbering machine to another friend, Carlos Glidden. Glidden watched the machine number the papers. Then he scratched his head.

"You can make a machine print numbers," he said. "So why can't you make one that writes letters?"

Sholes and Soulé had never thought of that. What a fine idea!

Soon the three men formed a partnership. Together they set out to invent a writing machine.

A few inventors had tried to make such a device. One as early as 1714. But no one had managed to print more than one letter of the alphabet. And even printing that much had been slower than writing with a pen.

The three inventors had no models to look at. None of the earlier inventors had left plans behind. Besides, only one had been an American. So even people who had seen those earlier inventions were hard to find.

The three men were often discouraged. Many times Soulé and Glidden wanted to stop and throw away all the strange-looking machines they had built. But Sholes would not give up. He pushed his partners to continue the work.

Finally, he built a sort of writing machine out of scraps of metal. Parts of his invention were even made of wood. But it only printed one letter—*W*. In fact, it could print a whole page of *W*s. But no one wanted that. Sholes went back to inventing.

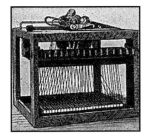

At last in 1867, he was very excited. He had developed a machine that produced all the letters of the alphabet. And it printed faster than a man or woman could write with a pen.

The machine Sholes built looked something like the modern typewriters. It had two rows of keys and a ribbon soaked with ink.

Sholes called to his two partners to come and see. He had something wonderful to show them.

They looked the machine over. Then Sholes proudly typed a message. It said

C. LATHAM SHOLES, SEPTEMBER 1867

Soulé and Glidden danced about the workshop. They were happy. Now they would be rich.

The three partners applied for and shared a patent. It would show that they had been first with this invention. They called it the "Type-writer."

But their work was not over. For six more years, they worked to make their machine better. No one could use it the way it was. Ink smeared over everything. The bars that moved the letters kept jamming. And the machine only printed capital letters.

Money was scarce. All three men borrowed from their families and friends. Soulé and Glidden became more and more discouraged. And they were more and more in debt.

Those two partners decided to give up. They both sold their shares of the patent to other investors. Because of this, Soulé and Glidden never made any money from the later success of the invention.

Sholes didn't do much better. He perfected his machine in 1873. Then he sold his rights for $6,000. It seemed like a great deal of money to him. The money equaled about eight or nine years' salary.

The Remington Company had bought him out. The typewriter would mean millions of dollars for them!

But Sholes was never bitter. He loved to play with his wonderful writing machine as he grew older. He never again wrote with a pen or pencil. He typed everything, including his signature, in the years before he died at the age of 71.

Some have called Christopher Latham Sholes the world's most unknown inventor. And with good reason.

The Wonderful Writing Machine Comes of Age

The Remington Company was known as the maker of guns and sewing machines before it bought the typewriter patent. In fact, one of their first typewriters was mounted on a sewing machine table.

The writer could not see the words on the first machines. The typist had to stop and roll the paper up to see how the writing looked. It also required great effort to push down the stiff keys.

When a line of typing was finished, the carriage was returned by stepping on a foot **treadle**. This was like the treadle used to operate a sewing machine.

Remington built 1,000 of these machines in 1873. The people who bought those first typewriters were often lawyers and writers.

One of the first to use the wonderful writing machine was Samuel Clemens. He wrote under the name Mark Twain. He was the author of *Tom Sawyer* and *Huckleberry Finn*.

Clemens sent his book *Life on the Mississippi* to his publisher as a typed manuscript. This was the first time any book had been submitted that way.

A Remington engineer invented a way to print lowercase letters in 1878. A new key, the *shift key*, was added. And the foot treadle was replaced by a carriage return. The typist's right hand moved it.

When Thomas Edison heard about the typewriter, he made a prediction. He said that someday the new machine would run on electricity. He had even built a model in 1871 that worked on magnets. But it was not a great success. And Edison lost interest in it.

Sholes had worried that his invention would be a fad. He hoped people would not stop using it. But, of course, he should not have worried. The machine became more and more popular. Doctors, newspaper people, clerks, and authors bought the machines in large numbers.

Sholes said, "I'm glad I had something to do with it. I built wiser than I knew."

TALKING over a WIRE

Alexander Bell was like his father and grandfather. He dreamed of teaching the deaf. He wanted to help them speak clearly. And he wanted to make their lives better.

Bell was born in Scotland in 1847. He and his two brothers were educated at home. His mother was nearly deaf. But she was a talented painter and musician. She taught her sons to play the piano. She also instructed them in grammar, spelling, reading, arithmetic, and art.

Although people had heard about electricity, it was not yet in their homes. So music was important to family life in those days.

Most family members learned to play the piano or some other musical instrument. Then the family would perform favorite songs together in the evenings. This was a much-loved way to pass the time after dark.

The Bells were a warm and loving family. But young Alexander was a worry to his parents. He was not a good student. Only a few subjects like the animal world interested him. And he liked to read and memorize plays and speeches. The rest of his lessons bored him.

Bell decided when he was 11 to change his name. It had been the same as his father's and grandfather's long enough. A family friend named Alexander Graham came to visit. Young Bell liked the name "Graham." So he decided to take it as part of his own.

"From now on, my full name will be Alexander Graham Bell," he said.

With his older brother, Melville, Bell studied how sounds were made. He also worked with his father on a system of pictures for the deaf called Visible Speech.

The pictures showed the positions of the tongue and lips for each sound. Visible Speech had already helped many deaf people learn to speak.

Bell began teaching the deaf using his father's Visible Speech system when he was 21 years old. He had never worked with deaf children before. But he had grown up in a home with a mother who could hear very little.

Bell knew of the special problems of speech for those who could not hear. And he knew more than most people about sound and how the vocal cords worked.

How he hoped he would be a successful teacher. If only he could help his students learn to speak!

Then tragedy struck. His younger brother, Edward, died of tuberculosis in 1867. Bell was lonely and filled with grief. He tried to fill his time. He taught classes in the evenings. Late at night, he studied, experimented, and read books about sound.

Following his long interest in animals, Bell decided to teach the family dog to "talk." He pushed and pressed the little terrier's mouth and throat. A series of growls came from the dog. They sounded a bit like human speech. The dog learned to say "ow, ah, ooh, ga, ma, ma." Bell insisted the dog had been asking "How are you, grand-ma-ma."

Tragedy came again two years later. Bell's infant nephew, who was never a strong baby, died suddenly. The baby's father, Melville, died a few months later of tuberculosis.

Bell and his parents were heartsick. The family thought a change of weather would be good for them. So they left Scotland in 1870. They sailed with Melville's widow to Quebec.

Young Bell was now 23. He helped his parents and sister-in-law settle in Canada. Then he traveled to Boston, Massachusetts. He had been invited to teach his father's Visible Speech methods there. Soon he became well known for his work with the deaf.

One of his pupils was an intelligent young woman named Mabel Hubbard. She was ten years younger than Bell. But the two came to love each other dearly.

Wanting to do more for deaf people like Mabel kept Bell interested in science. And Boston was a good place to learn.

Bell studied books about electricity and went to lectures at the Massachusetts Institute of Technology. He sat at home for hours at the piano, experimenting with sounds.

The telegraph sends dot and dash messages using electricity, Bell thought. Could there possibly be a way to send the sound of voices?

A telegraph wire could send only one message at a time in those days. Bell became interested in the **harmonic telegraph**, or multiple, line. But he was busy teaching all day. How could he find the answers? There was only one way. He began to experiment in the evenings.

Other men were also trying to make a successful harmonic telegraph. Bell rushed to be first. All the while, his experiments brought him closer to the idea of a telephone and how human voices might travel through a wire.

Bell needed money to do more work on the harmonic telegraph. He found two partners in the fall of 1874.

One was a pupil's father—a man named Sanders. The other was Gardiner Hubbard, Mabel's father. The three men formed the Bell Patent Association.

Sanders and Hubbard did not want Bell wasting his time working on his telephone dream. Their money was invested in the multiple telegraph. And that was where they wanted Bell's attention! The telephone would have to wait.

The partners hired Thomas Watson in the fall of 1874. He was to help Bell with the multiple telegraph. Right from the start, Bell and Watson got along well. Before long, they had built a working model of the improved telegraph.

An excited Bell hurried to Washington, D.C. He visited the nation's only telegraph company, Western Union. The company wanted a multiple telegraph. But they did not think his model was quite complete.

Bell continued with both inventions even though his partners insisted he work only on the telegraph. There was little time for sleep.

One June day in 1875, Watson was sending sound waves from the telephone **transmitter**. But part of the machine stuck. He plucked at it with his finger.

Bell was in the other room. He saw a metal reed move on his receiver. He rushed to Watson. "What did you do? Let me see!" he said excitedly.

The two men *were* very excited! The receiver's wire jiggled when the reed was plucked on the transmitter. And they could hear a sound like a human voice.

Bell and Watson moved their workroom to a boardinghouse early the next year. There they continued to improve the sound brought over their wire. Now the voice made their wire move up and down in a dish of acid mixed with water.

Suddenly, Bell cried out. "Mr. Watson! Come here! I want you!" He had spilled some burning acid on his clothes.

But this problem was soon forgotten. The two men realized how clearly Bell's voice had traveled over the wire.

Bell went to Philadelphia in June of 1876. He prepared an exhibit of his inventions for America's Centennial Exhibition. Mabel's brother, Willie, went along as Bell's assistant.

They spread the inventions on a long table. Next to them Bell tacked up a neatly lettered card. It read "Telegraphic and Telephonic Apparatus by A. Graham Bell."

The model Bell showed looked a little like a **megaphone** sitting on a wooden base. The receiver was a hollow iron cylinder three inches long. Inside was an iron rod wrapped with insulated copper wire. Bell and Willie strung a wire from the telephone on the table to a spot 100 yards away. Bell would send messages to the receiver from there.

The day was hot and the judges were very tired. Several had said they wanted to stop for the day. "We simply cannot continue in such heat!" they said.

They hadn't even looked at Bell's inventions.

He was frantic. He had to return to Boston to teach the next day. How could he explain his work if the judges quit?

Bell looked up to see one of the judges standing nearby. It was Emperor Dom Pedro from Brazil. Here was a friend. Bell had given copies of his father's Visible Speech book to this important visitor the week before.

Dom Pedro recognized Bell. The plump, cheerful emperor called the other judges over to the table. Mopping their brows, they gathered around. The emperor signaled them to sit down.

Bell showed his telephone. He explained how sound waves would flow with an **undulatory motion**. That is, they would vibrate in waves along the wire.

Bell hurried the 100 yards to the transmitter. The judges picked up the receiver one by one. Bell sang songs to some of them. To others, he recited a line from Shakespeare's play *Hamlet*. "To be or not to be, that is the question."

The judges were astonished. They quickly awarded Bell first prize.

An excited Bell hurried home to Boston. But not many people had heard about his prize. Or about his telephone. The newspapers weren't any help. They hardly mentioned Bell's work when they reported on the Centennial Exhibition.

Bell and Watson continued their work. They ran a test at the town's telegraph office. There they connected their telephone to the telegraph line. Bell hooked up his transmitter five miles away. He again recited Shakespeare. He sent a message long-distance for the first time.

A few months later, Bell and Watson developed a way to send messages in two directions on the same line. Now they were on their way to fame and fortune!

Bell and Watson spoke over a two-way line on October 9, 1876. That line was two miles long! It stretched across Boston's Charles River.

In December, their conversation traveled from Boston to Conway, New Hampshire. It was a distance of 143 miles!

Even Gardiner Hubbard agreed that Bell should stop working on his telegraph improvements. He must concentrate on perfecting the telephone. And Hubbard was very happy Mabel would be Bell's wife.

Alexander Graham Bell became wealthy and famous. Everyone wanted to use the telephone.

But when Bell was asked what in his life had made him most proud, he always gave the same answer. He wanted to be remembered as a teacher of the deaf.

chapter **9**

MESSAGES on the WING

Santa Catalina Island, off the coast of California, was well known by the early 1890s. The island was popular as a home for California's wealthy. The climate was nearly perfect.

Catalina was separated from Los Angeles by only 55 miles. And 26 miles of that was ocean. The rest was land.

Three boats daily crossed the water in summer. But there was only one boat in winter. And even that one sometimes was canceled due to bad weather. Telegraph communications did not yet pass between the island and the mainland.

The 5,000 residents of Catalina were worried. What if some emergency arose? How would they communicate? They took their worries to the Banning Company, owners of the island.

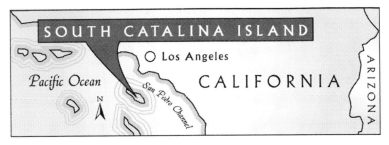

Two energetic brothers, Otto and Oswald Zahn, thought they might have the answer—carrier pigeons. "Why not take a chance?" the brothers asked. In 1894, the two men spent many weeks training a large flock of birds.

It was time at last for a test. A lead bird, named Orlando, left the island for Los Angeles. The hardy pigeon landed in the city in just over an hour. Such speed was amazing!

The messages were on 4" by 10" pieces of thin tissue paper. They were rolled into small bundles. Then they were attached with thread or a thin wire to the bird's leg or back.

Pigeon coops were set up on hilltops at Catalina and Los Angeles. When a bird arrived at a coop, a bell rang. It let the operator know there was a message.

The carrier pigeon service worked well for the residents of Catalina. This was sometimes not the case for the birds.

Any moment a hawk might swoop down upon a small pigeon. Most pigeon flights crossed over the same route almost every day. Whole flocks of hawks circled in those airspaces.

Hunters were another danger. They didn't know the importance of these trained pigeons. So these sportsmen often shot the birds as they passed overhead.

A wireless telegraph system was installed in 1902. It linked the island and the harbor town of San Pedro. No longer were the faithful carrier pigeons of Catalina needed. And no longer were they in danger.

10

chapter

MARCONI and the WONDERFUL WIRELESS

Guglielmo Marconi was born in 1874. He was the son of a wealthy Italian father and a strong, opinionated Irish mother.

His mother took Marconi to England when he was three years old. They visited his older brother who was in school there. Once there, his mother placed young Guglielmo in a private English preschool. They did not return to Italy for three years.

Once back in Italy, six-year-old Marconi faced a problem. He could speak almost no Italian. And what he did say was spoken with an English accent.

School was not a happy place for him. His Italian teachers had no patience with him. The boys at school teased him about the way he talked. He had few friends.

But Marconi had an inventive mind. He spent hours rigging up machines and experimenting with wires and batteries. He asked many questions of teachers and scientists.

Things improved for young Marconi when he was 13. His Italian had become better. Now no one teased him about the way he spoke. He had learned to sail a boat and had become a fine piano player.

His parents enrolled him in the Leghorn Technical Institute. There he had many chances to follow his interest in science. Soon he was studying physics and chemistry.

Electricity was a very exciting subject in those days. Marconi eagerly learned all he could. His mother saw this and paid for private lessons with well-known scientists.

Something important happened during this time. A German scientist named Heinrich Hertz built a transmitter. It caused a spark to jump from one metal bar to another. And there was no wire between. His work with such **electromagnetic waves** was of great interest in Germany.

But there was no way for young Marconi in Italy to learn about the work of Hertz in Germany. Scientific papers and books were not widely available.

Marconi received a shock when it came time to think of college. He failed to pass the entrance tests for the well-regarded Bologna University. His mother knew many important people there. But she did not have the power to get him into the university.

She did, however, arrange for him to use the laboratories and library there. And she continued to find tutors for her son. One of these was a retired telegraph operator who taught him Morse code.

Marconi was vacationing in the Alps in 1894. He was at a location close to Germany. Hertz had just died. And the newspapers had stories of his work with electromagnetic waves.

Marconi was fascinated with the idea of sending messages without wires. For days, he forgot his vacation and stayed in his room. All he wanted to do was think about sound waves.

I believe I can make that idea work, he thought. Messages without wires!

Marconi returned to Italy. His mother cleared two large rooms on the top floor of their house. He turned to Italy's most famous expert on electromagnetic waves for help.

"I had failed to use such waves after trying for many years," Professor Righi told Marconi. "Why do you think a young man can do this? Especially one who has not gone to college."

But Marconi would not give up. He was determined to use Hertzian sound waves to send messages. He did not know that an Englishman named Oliver Lodge had already done this. But Lodge had lost interest. And he had not applied for a patent.

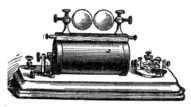
Marconi continued to work. Near the end of 1894, he called his mother into his workshop. She stood fascinated as he demonstrated his transmitter. He pressed a key at one end of the attic, and a buzzer sounded at the other end. There were no wires. Marconi's message had traveled 30 feet! Encouraged, he began to extend the distances for his experiments.

His father had often called Marconi "a useless son." But he was now interested in his son's work. He and his friends provided money for the wireless. Marconi's mother wrote to her friends in England. That country was interested. Marconi and his mother sailed to London in February of 1896.

Marconi at last applied for a patent in London. Then he began to work with the English Post Office. He planned a demonstration.

Marconi sent a message in Morse code for more than a mile. It traveled from one post office building to another. Those watching were shocked. The message traveled without wires. And there were several tall buildings between the two post offices. They didn't even block the signal.

Larger and larger areas were used for demonstrations. Marconi demonstrated his invention for England's newspapers and the general public in December 1896. And in May 1897, he first showed how such messages could be sent over 8.7 miles of water.

Marconi became famous for the wireless. Now messages could travel where wires could not be used. For example, they could go from a ship to the shore.

His English backers set up a company, "The Wireless Telegraph and Signal Company." Marconi gave the company the rights to his patent. And he became a director. He also received 60 percent of the company shares and $25,000 in cash.

He had been working on his invention for three years. He was rich. Scientists all over the world knew of his work. And he was only 23 years old!

The radios we use in our homes today are a form of Marconi's grand invention.

Marconi's Narrow Escape

Marconi and his wife received a special invitation in 1912. The world's greatest ocean liner was the *Titanic*. It was to make a maiden voyage across the Atlantic Ocean. This was a famous ship because it was thought to be unsinkable.

But there was a tragedy. The ship went down with 1,500 passengers and crew. Some 700 more might have died. But a radio message brought the liner *Carpathia* to the rescue.

Where were the Marconis? An important business appointment in the United States had caused Marconi to change his travel plans. He sailed on another ship. His wife canceled her *Titanic* ticket at the last minute because their two-year-old son was ill.

From Marconi's Wireless to the Home Radio

Dr. Ernest Alexanderson was an engineer for the General Electric Company. He built a transmitter that changed the "dit" and "dah" signals of the wireless into the sound of a human voice. The first demonstration carried the voice of Alexanderson's associate, Professor R. A. Fessenden, in December 1906.

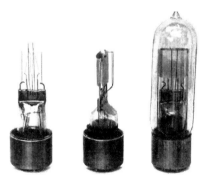

John Fleming was an English electrical engineer. He used some findings of Thomas Edison to develop new radio devices called **vacuum tubes**. Fleming's device turned **alternating current** into **direct current**. But his vacuum tube was bulky, expensive, and easily broken.

Lee De Forest was an American inventor. He improved Fleming's device. His **triode** made a far more powerful copy of the audio signal. It would be several years before the vacuum tube was perfected for general use. But the day of voice radio was coming ever closer.

Edwin Armstrong was a young graduate student from Columbia University. He developed the feedback circuit to **amplify** sound hundreds of times. He discovered in 1912 that a triode could be used not only to amplify signals but to generate them.

A **crystal receiver** used minerals. They worked well for voice reception. These receivers became popular with **ham radio operators** in the early 1900s. But the output from the crystals worked on a small amount of power and could not be amplified.

The days of the individual inventor working alone or with one or two assistants was almost over. Many scientists were working on the development of the radio. Some had their own companies. Others worked for large corporations.

The largest and best-known of all was still the Marconi Company. And Marconi was only in his thirties. But Marconi still wanted to build a vast worldwide wireless system. He wanted to send radio signals over greater and greater distances.

"Others could work with radio voice transmission," declared Marconi.

chapter 11

AMERICA CALLING, Are You There?

Theodore N. Vail said very little that day in Georgia. In fact, he spoke only 22 words. But the nation waited a long time to hear them.

Great advances in communication came to the United States in the 1880s. Bell's 1876 invention of the telephone had led to several important events.

First there was a two-way conversation. It traveled over a distance of two miles. Then came the first commercial long-distance line in 1881. It stretched 45 miles.

Before long, forward-looking businesses used the remarkable new invention. And telephones could often be seen in the private homes of the wealthy.

Theodore Vail, first president of the giant American Telephone and Telegraph Company (AT&T), had a dream. It was a plan that would quicken the pulse of the nation.

Chicago had been connected by telephone to the East Coast in 1892. Then Denver was hooked up in 1911. Now 1915 was almost here.

Vail felt sure his company could cross the length of the entire nation. He dreamed of a **network** of lines from New York to San Francisco. He ordered work to begin.

Vail planned a ceremony for the big day. He thought about it during the months needed to complete the project.

Alexander Graham Bell would place a call from New York. Thomas Watson would answer in San Francisco. President Woodrow Wilson would join the hookup in Washington, D.C.

Vail himself planned to join in on another New York line located in his office.

Vail waited while crews laid the needed miles of line across the western United States. He traveled south while the work continued. He had been invited by friends to vacation at the exclusive Millionaire's Club. The club was on Jekyll Island just offshore from Brunswick, Georgia. He enjoyed the social whirl of dinners, picnics, and sports with America's richest families.

As luck would have it, he suffered an injury to his leg. Now he needed many weeks of healing.

He hobbled impatiently about the island. He was angry and frustrated. And he worried about his bad luck. His lameness would prevent his return to New York.

"I will not be left out of such an important telephone call!" he vowed.

Vail ordered the ceremony postponed. The celebration would have to wait. He would be part of that phone call!

Vail's company would just have to string an additional 1,000 miles of wire. Then Jekyll Island would be hooked up with New York, Washington, D.C., and San Francisco.

The workmen would have to hurry! A deadline for the history-making call across the nation was set for January 25, 1915.

Vail's crews worked overtime. They strung a special line from Savannah, Georgia, to Brunswick. Then they met another challenge. They had to get across the marshy channel to Jekyll Island.

At one point, a tree fell across the wire. All work stopped while an emergency crew repaired the break.

The telephone crewmen finally were near the island. But they ran into trouble again. Security guards wanted to know what were they doing with a boat filled with coils of cable? No strangers were allowed on Jekyll. They were refused permission to land.

Vail had to be contacted immediately. He and his host had to give permission before the work crew could step onto the island.

All was ready at last. Bell waited in New York. Watson was in San Francisco. President Wilson was on the line in Washington. Gathered around him were members of the National Geographic Society, an organization that Bell had helped form. On Jekyll Island, Vail sat with his ankle propped on a pillow. He fiddled with his headset.

First Bell spoke to his old friend, Watson. He used the words he first sent back in 1876. "Mr. Watson! Come here! I want you!"

Watson answered from the West Coast. With a laugh, he said, "It would take a week for me to do that now."

President Wilson joined the call a few moments later. He praised Bell and Watson for their work.

Then he learned Vail was waiting on the line. The president started a new conversation. "This is the President. I have just been speaking across the continent."

"Oh, yes." Vail said his first words.

"Before I give up the telephone, I want to extend my congratulations to you. This has been a remarkable work," continued the president.

"Thank you," answered Vail.

"I am sorry to hear that you are sick," the president said.

"I am getting along well. I am sort of a cripple, that's all."

"I hope you will be well soon. Good-bye, Mr. Vail."

"Thank you. Good-bye, Mr. President."

It was a simple conversation. Some might wonder if Vail's 22 words were worth all the expense. And all the effort.

The telephone call is well remembered on Jekyll Island. On a broad lawn near the Rockefeller mansion, a small stand holds a model of the original telephone. A plaque under it tells about the occasion.

The first transcontinental telephone call was a major event for this small island in the shallow waters off Georgia.

chapter

RADIO COMES to the AMERICAN HOME

The United States entered World War I in 1917. This led to further development of the radio.

Generals and admirals used it to communicate how and where to move their armies and fleets. Scientists worked day and night during the war years to develop better radio equipment.

Peace came in 1918. Radio equipment had been made more powerful, compact, and affordable. Now it was time to reach out to the American people.

Some private citizens were already building their own sets. They called themselves *hams*. And they spent hours talking into their transmitters.

Dr. Frank Conrad, an engineer for Westinghouse Company, sent messages to ham radio operators in 1920. He asked the hams to help with some experiments.

Conrad began playing phonograph records for the hams between his voice messages. The hams liked this idea! "Thank you, thank you," they said.

News of the radio broadcasts spread. Soon a downtown store had set up a radio receiver to entertain customers.

A Westinghouse Company vice president wondered if the public would listen to a full-time broadcast. He ordered Conrad to set up a radio station on the roof of one of the company's warehouses.

KDKA went on the air on November 2, 1920. It was the world's first commercial radio station. Americans were wild with exciteme

They rushed to buy radios for their homes. About 7.5 million radio sets had been sold in the United States by 1927.

The Great Depression began in 1929. This disaster helped the spread of radio. It's true, Americans had very little money to spend on radio sets. But as soon as a family bought one, they had continuing entertainment.

There was no need to go outside the home and spend money. Listeners could now hear fast-breaking news as soon as it happened. Radio comedies, plays, and variety shows brightened the evenings. President Franklin Delano Roosevelt spoke to the people during his "fireside chats." Radio, as a communications invention, had come into its own.

"Radio," Americans told one another, "is wonderful. The only thing better would be if we could see the person who's speaking." As you might guess, inventors were already working on this next step.

Leaders on the Road to Television

Vladimir Zworykin was a Russian scientist. He hoped to find a way to use cathode-ray tubes to send pictures.

The Communists took over Russia in 1917. So he fled to the United States. He worked for the Westinghouse Company and then for the Radio Corporation of America (RCA). World War II slowed down his inventing.

But soon peace came. RCA went ahead with his ideas for both the television camera and the television set.

Philo Taylor Farnsworth worked on an idea for a television system. He had no money to finish his education at the University of Utah. But he managed to interest some businessmen in his work with cathode-ray tubes.

His invention, the **image dissector**, cleared up the shadows and black dots that had appeared on Zworykin's screen. He was only 24 when he registered his first patents. And he continued his inventing throughout his lifetime.

Farnsworth made improvements to radar and invented the first fax machine before his death in 1971.

chapter 13

TELEVISION COMES
to the AMERICAN HOME

Television was a new invention that arrived at an unfortunate time. Many Americans could afford to buy a small radio during the Depression. But almost no one could manage to own an expensive television. Only about 10,000 television sets had been sold in the entire country by the end of the 1930s.

Millions of people first saw television at the New York World's Fair in 1939. A great many were interested in owning their own sets.

But World War II began. And parts used to make television sets were needed to supply communication equipment for the military.

Most servicemen had returned home by the late 1940s. Television became something most Americans could now own. About ten million TV sets were in American homes by 1951.

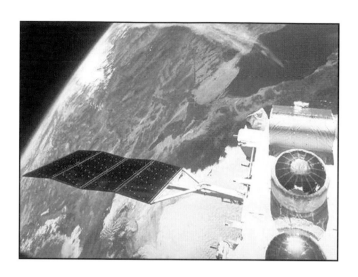

Cable and Satellites Send the Television Picture

Television became a common thing for the American family. But there were still some who could not receive its signal.

Television signals worked like light rays. They traveled in a straight line. They could not jump over mountains and tall buildings. Weather conditions could ruin transmission. People who lived far out in the country often couldn't get television at all.

The **coaxial cable** solved those problems. The cable was a combination of crowded wires in a tube. It was expensive to lay the cable between cities. But slowly it became popular because of the fine picture it offered.

Later, television signals were reflected off satellites. This solved transmission problems caused by mountains, buildings, and bad weather.

Television signals were sent into space, received by the satellite, and beamed back to anywhere in the world. This type of television reception grew more popular. And the size of the **dish** needed to bring in the signal grew smaller and easier to install.

chapter 14

A SMALL IDEA That GREW and GREW

The earliest computers in America were so big that each one filled a room. Only the largest companies used them.

Personal computers were not used as a communication tool even when they became available for homes. Each computer owner worked alone.

For a long time, there was no way to send a message to someone else's computer. It was some time before inventors decided to work together. Perhaps they might find a way to link computers—something like a net.

A group of men gathered on the college campus of the University of California at Los Angeles (UCLA) in 1969. Their idea was a new one. Perhaps they could develop an engineering project. They needed a special plan to allow computers to talk to one another.

Their leader was Professor Leonard Kleinrock. "Once we start our work," he told the 40 other scientists, "we'll try to get into the information systems of one another's computers." This was a brand-new idea.

Men would try to cut across individual companies to exchange information for the first time. This was a big step for science and for business.

No one expected to produce anything that might be used by the average American.

The government was looking for better ways to use its funds for computer research. Computer systems had made different levels of progress. For example, UCLA was known for its fine simulations. The University of Utah led the way in graphics.

How much better the government's money could be used if all the discoveries could be shared! The government officials suggested some type of network where universities could share their knowledge.

Four centers were connected in September 1969. They were UCLA, the University of Utah, University of California at Santa Barbara (UCSB), and Stanford University. Professor Kleinrock was appointed as chairman of the project.

When the four universities had been connected, Kleinrock gave the command. "Log in," he said.

Suddenly, the network crashed. Right after the letter *O* was entered. Fortunately, the programmers had the network up and running again in just a few hours.

Soon a **node** was set up at UCLA. It was a big switch the size of a telephone booth! It provided for the hookup with other universities. The first telecommunications network had been born!

The scientists were excited by this progress. But they still never pictured a system that would involve home computers. In fact, these men in 1969 could not imagine that private citizens might *want* computers in their homes!

There was a clue, though. The first email was entered on the screens of the joint university system in 1972. The response was immediate. Such people-to-people communication was what all the university scientists wanted. Soon the term *Internet* was being heard around the campus computer centers.

Interconnected computers became wildly popular. Research labs from private companies soon applied for hookup to the university systems.

Students who had worked with Professor Kleinrock were beginning to move all over the world. Networking and research centers started up wherever they went.

Recently, Kleinrock was quoted as saying that he now can picture a world where every building in America will have a computer in it. And all will be connected to the Internet at all times.

The world and the Internet have come a long way since Professor Kleinrock's meeting in 1969.

COMMUNICATION TODAY

Do you remember Running Stag, the American Indian? Do you remember his son, Little Deer? Think what they would see if they came to your school today.

They would see a postal worker delivering letters to the school office. Telephones would ring. The secretary would work at a computer. A fax machine would bring messages. Perhaps the secretary would call the principal to the office using a beeper or cell phone.

In the classroom, you and your friends might be watching a television program about science. Students at individual computers would do research on the Internet. Others would write letters and reports or send email to their friends.

What might Running Stag think? What would be going through the head of Little Deer?

We can only imagine.

GLOSSARY

alternating current   movement of electricity that reverses its direction at regular intervals

amplify   to increase or expand

cathode ray   energy that passes from a nonmetallic to a metallic conductor

coaxial cable   tube of copper or other conducting material. The center is another conductor. They are separated by insulation. This cable allows for a large number of telegraph and telephone messages, as well as television images, to be sent at the same time.

crystal receiver   device that is powered only by the radio waves it picks up; needs no electrical source. A tiny gemlike material in the electric circuit makes the radio sensitive to radio waves.

daguerreotype   early way of processing photographs on a silver or a silver-colored plate

direct current   movement of electricity that moves in one direction only

dish   device for receiving radio, television, and other electronic signals from satellites in space

electromagnetic wave   motion caused by periodic variation of electric and magnetic intensity happening at the same time; includes radio waves, infrared rays, visible light, ultraviolet light, X rays, and gamma rays

franking   system in which certain people can send mail free of charge

ham radio operator   person who builds and runs his or her own radio station as a hobby

hardtack   saltless hard biscuit, bread, or cracker

harmonic telegraph   system that allows more than one message to travel on a wire

image dissector   device that produces a clear, visible image on a screen

61

isthmus	narrow strip of land connecting two larger land areas
megaphone	cone-shaped device used to increase the volume of the voice
mica	variety of shiny, colorful minerals
network	system of lines, wires, channels, and communication lines that links groups together
node	point where everything centers; main link
receiver	device for receiving and changing signals into audio or visual form
rotunda	large round room
semaphore	system for visual signaling with two flags, one in each hand
snowshoes	light oval frames that are strung with thongs. They are attached to the feet so a person can walk on soft snow without sinking.
tinder	material used to start a fire
tinker	to work with something in an experimental manner
transcontinental	extending or going across a continent
transmitter	device for sending audio or visual signals
treadle	a foot-powered pedal or lever that makes a machine work
triode	kind of vacuum tube; can increase a weak signal
undulatory motion	wavy movement caused by the vibration of different tones
vacuum tube	sealed glass or metal container from which almost all air has been removed. It controls the electric currents called *electronic signals*. These signals are necessary for radios, television sets, and computers. Most vacuum tubes have been replaced by smaller devices called *transistors*. A TV screen is one end of a vacuum tube.

INDEX